WORDS FROM ONE

By

Brian Graham

Words from One
Brian Graham

Published by Greyhound Self-Publishing 2016
Malvern, Worcestershire, United Kingdom.

Printed and bound by Aspect Design
89 Newtown Road, Malvern, Worcs. WR14 1PD
United Kingdom
Tel: 01684 561567
E-mail: allan@aspect-design.net
Website: www.aspect-design.net

A copy of this book has been deposited with the British Library Board

ISBN: 978-1-909219-42-7

FORWARD

So, what exactly is One Word Verse?

One Word Verse is when you take a word as the title of the poem and write something related to its meaning using only the letters that appear in that word.

The maximum number of letters allowed is nine.

For example, 'Rainbows' has eight different letters, so using only these letters and no others, you write something about Rainbows.

'Cappuccino' has seven different letters; c,a,p,u,i,n,o, so you use only these letters to write something about Cappuccino.

Lionel Shorstone has fifteen letters but only nine different ones and so this is fine.

The eagle-eyed among you may have noticed that 'Lionel Shorstone' is two words and that the title of the book suggests only One can be used. Not to worry. I can't help but think it is within the boundaries of artistic license to use more than One word, even though this does not actually stand up to scrutiny. The important thing is to set yourself a limit on how many letters are permitted. Nine is good for me.

If you feel inspired to try this One Word Verse caper yourself, I wish you good luck and plenty of enjoyment.

The way I usually approach it is to write down as many words as I can see from the letters which make up the title, scan the words to see if any pattern evolves and take it from there. For you, same same but different? The chances are that with a lot of titles you will use only a fraction of the words that are available to you. What is revealed in your verse may reveal something about the nature of how your mind works.

Warm wishes

Brian Graham

This is the first One Word Verse I ever read out to an audience.

It was at a Confab Cabaret gig at the Mount Pleasant Hotel just over the road from Abbey Road Coffee in Really Great Malvern not so long ago.

It is dedicated to overcoming fear.

RAINBOWS

I saw Brian's brain born in air, soar,

as an arrow in a bow.

So, now, Brian's brain is in a Rainbow.

A Rainbow woos, soon wins.

So, now, Brian is a Rainbow Warrior..

Wow !

'Wow' Indeed!

"So," I almost hear you ask, "Where does the inspiration for all this unique One Word Verse come from?"

The answer might surprise you. The inspiration comes from the cappuccino. Yes, the humble and ubiquitous cappuccino. Not just any cappuccino though, but one of those I have just about every day sitting outside the Abbey Road Coffee in Really Great Malvern. And so this is my ode to the cappuccino.

CAPPUCCINO

Can I cap a Cappuccino?

No!

Can a nap?

No!

Can a nun on a piano?

No!

Can a cop on a nun on a piano?

O, No, No, No!!!

O Cappuccino!

No pain.

No panic.

No poo.

Cappuccino;

A union

A coup!

Ciao!

"So, if inspiration comes from the cappuccino, where does inspiration come from; in and of itself?" I almost hear you asking yourselves. Well, you might not be altogether wrong if you replied

"From the eight different letters that make up the word 'Inspiration' "

So, this is what happened when I put this theory to the test and, it must be admitted, with somewhat surprising results. However, I like to think that this can be attributed to the diversity of the gathering I addressed, rather than me getting a little bit carried away with myself. This is a transcript of how things transpired when I posed the question.

INSPIRATION

Torpor?

Sit!

Aspirants, narrators, tip top orators,
rapportists, satirists 'n' ripostants...

Stop.

Sit.

Sit 'n' sip port.

Sit 'n' sip port as I posit (not parrot!)

‘Sir, Inspiration isn’t a sport. It isn’t a sport star. It’s not...’

‘Stan, sit! No opposition,’ I insist.

‘Pronto, sit.

Sit ‘n’ sip port as I pass potions into a pot.’

Tara:

‘Inspiration isn’t a piss poor artist.

It’s not Paris.

It not a pianist in rain atop a tor

‘n’ it ain’t Tarantino!’

Stan:

‘It’s not a pint ‘n’ it’s not a nip!

Stan! It’s not a nap!

Stan; It’s not a nap. Sip port!!!!!’

Tina:

‘It isn’t Santa.

Nor is it Satin pants.

It’s not Tonto or Tintin

‘n’ pssssstt! It ain't Panto too!’

Nan:

‘Is it as aspirin is to pain?

Or as it isn’t?’

St Ninian:

‘Isn’t it!’

Rasta:

‘It isn’t roots ‘n’ it isn’t toot.

’n’ it is, ‘n’ it isn’t.

Innit!’

Spa:

‘It isn’t Rap’s rants ‘n’ strops ‘n’ it isn’t pants.

Or is it?’

(Stan, ‘Sit ‘n’ sip port!

Stan, It’s not a nap!’)

Pat:

'It isn't pro rata or rotas or rostas.

It isn't train stations or airports or passports.

It's not notations or annotations.

It's not stats.

Or is it?'

Sartra:

'Is it troops, riots, assassinations, paranoia, pain 'n' rapists? Is it?

Sartra! It is in sin 'n' it isn't in sin!'

Pan:

'Is it tarot's propositions

as Pi appoints stars in top positions

or is it an apparition?'

Sita:

'To Trappists, it's a prostration.

To Saints, it's Narnia.

To Taoists...It is as it is'

'So, Aspirants.

Apropos to torpor.

Apropos to Inspiration.

A tip

It isn't...'

('Stan! Sip port! It's NOT a nap!)

'A tip.

It isn't a sit in.

It isn't sippin' port.

It's not stop or start.

It's not a sprint into or topspin

'n' it ain't a.s.a.p.

It's not a trait.

It's not art.

It's not apart.

It's not a   part.

So, sit ‘n’ sip port.

As I strap it in.

As I appoint it.

As I anoint it.

As I soar into.

As I attain,

An apt instant nano astro intra strata initiation into notion transitions in ...

Roast potato rotations !!!

p.s.

Print it ‘n’ pass it on to Stan.’

You might also be interested to read the transcript of the conversation I had with Stan the next day:

SYNTHESIS

‘This thesis is shit.’

‘No it isn’t.’

‘ Yes it is. It’s shit!’

Which I found to be a little uncouth to say the least and is a reminder of how it is so difficult to find a good audience nowadays.

Oh well, moving on swiftly... It has been said of Buddhists that, perhaps, because of belief in reincarnation, we tend to take the longer term view of life. The following is a verse dedicated to opening the mind to being able to look at something from a way other than we have a tendency to. It is also dedicated to the Mystery.

HIEROS GAMOS *

* Greek: The sacred union of the masculine and feminine.

Om

Rare memories…

I roam ashore

so ego rises;

arises as he, arises as she.

As ego arises,

a sea shimmies.

Osmosis arises,

Eros emerges,

Eros immerses as she;

Immerses as he.

Sea shimmies.
Sea marries he; marries she.
marries ego; marries eros.
Shares me.

Sages agree, memories are One.
So, ami, amie, aim high.
As memories merge; share memories...so
memories re-emerge as Hieros Gamos;
as memories
Are Hieros Gamos.
Are Om.
Are Home.
Are One.

Hmm! Very interesting. Very interesting Indeed! And brings us very nicely indeed to more recent times.

Now then (Then now?), those of you blessed with having been to Really Great Malvern may be aware of a boutique just over the road from Abbey Road Coffee. It is on Belle Vue Terrace and goes through life with the name of 'Iapetus'. What you may not be aware of, however, is that

Iapetus is named after the Iapetus sea which had its shoreline on North Hill in the Malvern Hills 325 million years ago.

So, there I was 325 million years ago, standing on the North Hill shoreline, staring out to sea while pondering over the meaning of life, when suddenly a storm blew up over the Iapetus and the letters of Iapetus rearranged themselves to give me an answer of sorts.

Iapetus

Iapetus is a sea.

It's upset.

It is as it is.

It passes.

At ease it is us.

So what happens next? Only that 325 million years later, I am back on the North Hill, staring out over the Worsaucester valley, when I have a past life memory. Again, it is the letters of Iapetus rearranging themselves for me and providing me with a clue to the mysteries of life; this time, a more updated one.

Iapetus is a sea.

It's upset.

As I see past it, it sets.

I see it is us.

I suss us at ease.

'Hmmm', I almost hear you say. "Very good but do you not think that maybe you are leaving yourself open to the danger of being criticised as being perceived as being somewhat nostalgic?"

Well, for sure for sure for sure 4 sure, this is not outside the realms of possibility but it does bring to mind the question 'What exactly is meant by 'Nostalgia?'

Maybe there is an inherent answer to be found in the eight letters that make up this contentious word?

As a wise person once said

'Let's see'

NOSTALGIA

Is Nostalgia a sign?

Is it going on 'n' on 'n' on?

Is it aging?

Is it stagnation?

Is it anal?

Is it a gloss?
A gain, a loss?
Alas, it is 'n' it isn't.

It isn't
G 'n' Ts 'n' Santa,
Galags 'n' Glasnost,
Latin 'n' Atlantis,
Tinto 'n' Tonto.

It is
Initiations in Goa.
It's ting 'n' ting in I 'n' I* gigs.
It's lino 'n' loons 'n' losing lists
It's "Goooo on" 'n' singing.
It's again, initiations in Goa, again.

Nostalgia is long ago
And not so long ago.
It's also soon.
Soon; as in....

Logging on 'n' Installations

Logos, tagging 'n' litigation.

It's L.O.L. Innit!

So, Nostalgia is as it is.

All in all, Nostalgia is all it is.

It's Aligning.

It's all Aligning.

* Loosely 'God' - Rastafarian

"Well, well, well", as the man said when he saw the three holes in the ground. That was very interesting, very interesting indeed. Not only does it give an insight into Buddhist views of time, it's also an intriguing way of spelling 'go' when you said "Gooooo on". It suggests you are a Brummy and that it tickles you in some way to sometimes spell a word in the way that you pronounce it, or, 'phonetically' as some good people might say."

And do you know what dear readers? You would be absolutement correct in this line of thinking. I am, indeed from the Motherland (Handsworth, but more of that later) and the reason why this change of spelling tickles me is that you need to have a Brummy accent in order to ask yourself two very profound questions and to make them rhyme…

What d'ya think you're doing?

And where d'ya think you're goooing?

On a more prosaic level, the place I am often goooing to when I leave the Temple is Abbey Road Coffee which takes one cigarette if I walk slowly or a little longer if I dawdle. One of the baristas of the Abbey Road Coffee is Cameron, an Australian gentleman who segues seamlessly between being an Old Soul and also bringing to life some of those qualities of finesse and subtlety for which Australians are world famous. Cam is also a professional musician and I have had the pleasure of watching him 'at it' with his voice and his guitar. So this is dedicated to Cameron at a time when he had just finished a gig at the 'Malvern Lounge' next door to the Abbey Road Coffee.

CAMERON

" More, More!

Come on Cam, Encore!

O man, once more!

One more Encore!"

Cam came on

Cam; no mere crooner.

No mere cameo Romancer.

Cam; a Necromancer!

Cam came on.

A roar; a Manna roar.

An Amora roar!

Cam; no mere man!

Cam; an Emanance.

Can a cancan mean more?

No!

Cam; a core Amen!

Cor!

Cameron

Om.

A. Moron

Sat outside the Abbey Road Coffee, with my Cappuccino as is my wont, I am able to observe a veritable multitude of little adventures, not least of which was the unexpected arrival of six large flowerpots not so long ago next to my table. They run the length of the passage from the steps adjacent to the Abbey Road Coffee, past Aquarius where I have a wee job of warning Val the owner that it looks like rain so she can bring the clothes in, and then past the Malvern Bookshop, ending up outside Hunky Dorey at the entrance to the Priory cemetery.

I like to think that I am also a silent sitting sentinel for both the Bookshop and for Hunky Dorey. And so it is that it is, that the next verse is a wee dedication to life as seen by these flowerpots; my constant Cappuccino companions and unsung heroes.

FLOWERPOTS

Ello!

We're Flowerpots.

We sport pert wee flowers.

We oft see wee flow too.

We peep, we peer.

We see steps.

We woo strollers.

Woo troopers.

We toot twerps.

We wow pets too!

So, We're Flowerpots.

We tell off woofers.

We stop fools.

We[i] wrestle; we floor pests.

We opt to see off trolls too.

We're Flowerpots.

We're spot on.

We rest. We sleep.

Or else, we powwow

or we tell walls woppers!

We tweet trees too!

We're flowerpots

We weep.

We follow Reporters

so we're O.T.T. too.

p.s.

We're Flowerpots.

"Blimey Bri." I almost hear you say. "There really does seem to be lots happening along this passageway down to the Priory. Out of all the things you've observed, sat there with your cappuccino, is there one incident that stays in your mind more than others?"

Oh, I don't really have any idea what stays in the mind and what doesn't, but there have been so many magical little moments sat outside Abbey Road Coffee that it sometimes feels as if they all blend in together. I would say, however, that I was very glad to be lingering in the doorway one autumnal afternoon and be party to Roo, another barista beau and guitarist with the White Feather Collective, showing a bit of class. And so it is that it is, that this verse is dedicated to Roo.

ABBEY ROAD COFFEE

Order Order!

Ready?

Dora, a broody Babe, ordered

"Free food. Free Coffee!"

Roo offered Dora a free cocoa.

" Cocoa? F. OFF! " roared Dora.

" Aye, a cocoa before bed" dared Roo!

Dora eyed Roo.

"Cor Roo! Cocoa! O do, do, do, Roo!"

Roo, ready, obeyed.

ordered a cab,

robbed cocoa (decaff)

robbed a carafe.

"Bye Dora. Bye Roo!"

For Roo, a bearded bard, adored Dora.

Dora, a rare Fab, Ace Babe, adored Roo.

Yabbadabbadoooooo!

Abbey Road Coffee, as the name suggests, sells coffee. It also sells wine but not Lumbresco, the fizzy one, which, for some reason, reminds me of kids at weddings being allowed to drink alcohol for the first time while being carefully watched over by their parents. It is not a drink associated with the street homeless. Yet, such is the undercurrent of diversity of Really Great Malvern, that I have had some conversations with a couple of street homeless people who appeared in RGM for a few weeks and who have now, as far as I am aware, moved on. Their tipple of choice was Lumbresco.

LUMBRESCO

Some sombre locals cuss us.
Some see bums.
See losers.
See cumbersome users.
Some see less.

Some see more;
See us source Lumbresco
See Lumbresco rescues us.
Some see Lunbresco's summer sombreros.
See us rebel.
See us sober.
See us blossom.

So, more or less,
Remember Lumbresco,

Remember Souls,

Remember us,

Remember me.

Om.

Somebody else who has moved on is my friend, Lionel Shorstone. I was outside Abbey Road Coffee one day writing a letter to a friend, Michaela, when Lionel, a Druid, facilitator of the local Interfaith group, which I regularly attend and organizer of Malvern's burgeoning Well Blessing ceremonies, walked past and joined me at the table.

I only knew Lionel slightly at the time. When he left half an hour later, I continued with my letter and vividly remember penning how I was now feeling a warm glow about myself. This, I put down to being in Lionel's presence for that short time. This is Lionel all over.

From here on in, we would meet up every Wednesday morning at Abbey Road Coffee where we would chew the cud. These conversations were always a delight and will not be forgotten. The following is what I read out at his funeral; the celebration of his life.

LIONEL SHORSTONE

I sense Lionel in the Hills.
In the trees.
In the stones.
I sense Lionel in the ether.
Herein, therein, lies Lionel.

I sense
No Loneliness.
No tensions.
No toil.
I sense Lionel shines still.

I sense
in Oneness he nestles.
I sense
Oneness is his nest.

His roots in the Hills.
His roots in the Ether.

In He.

In She.

In Entireties.

In Eternities.

I sense Lionel,

I sense Lionel Shorstone.

Michaela, my friend who I was writing the letter to when Lionel walked in, is German and we have been handwriting letters to each other for almost 20 years. When I moved to Great Malvern, not so long ago, I wrote to her with my new address here and added the 'Really' to 'Great Malvern'. All the letters from Michaela have this extended address on the envelope and are always delivered by the Post Office; a verification of the truth of the matter should one ever be needed.

Anyway, I have also had 3 beautiful German girlfriends in my life which means that there is a big place in my heart for Germany. Therefore, the following prayer for Peace relates to the seemingly never ending global refugee crises which are becoming so much more of a feature closer to home; both on the physical level and the heart level.

GERMANY

Agree an arena, any arena.
Agree an age, any age.
Marry!
Me?
Germany!

May Germany manage,
manage a menage.
Emerge rare,
Merge many a year.

May a meme emerge
May Manna emerge
May an Anam* emerge
May Germany re -emerge

May Germany
Nary anger
Nary rage

Nary renege.

May Germany, a name, mean a merger.
May Germany, a name,
mean merry energy, eager.

Agree an arena, any arena.
Agree an age, any age.
Marry.
Me?
Germany!

* Soul (Gaelic)

On the theme of refugees; a while back, I spent some time at the refugee camp in Dunkirk, not far from Calais, which has since been demolished. I found myself completely out of my depth while I was there. However, what has become apparent to me in the aftermath, is that Love is never completely extinguished and so this next verse is dedicated to the Really Great Malvern organisation 'People in Motion' who organise things so that volunteers are able to go to the camps and help out as best they can. People in Motion is propelled by empathy and generosity of spirit.

This verse is also dedicated to the refugees I met who

revealed to me the most noble of qualities humanity has to offer. It is also dedicated to all those amongst us who are Refugees of one kind or another.

PEOPLE IN MOTION

Timeline

Mile 'pon mile, People in tent.

Not in loop.

No option imminent.

Til people in loop, no option loomin'.

No ....One Moment!

One Option.

One Notion.

Peep in tent; Meet me.

I not item.

I 'n' I People.

Peep in tent

in Intention, Intention, Intention!

Pool Intent.

Pool People Intent

Til I 'n' I in loop,

Til I 'n' I in Motion,

Til People in Motion.

People in Motion. People in Motion.

Penelope Om

Maybe that verse would sound better as dub reggae, but 'mustn't grumble' because back in Really Great Malvern, Paul Vlismas

VLISMAS

Alas, I amass saliva

vis a vis Villaisms

Another Villa fan! Eh? Aston Villa Football Club! Or Paul the Bookie, who used to work at the Malvern Bookshop with Rebecca two doors down from Abbey Road Coffee. He is an erudite gentleman who looks like an aging rock star would like to look. It was Paul who first introduced me to the word 'Doggerel'. The word is one which is used by erudite people when they look down on written words as being not quite worthy of their attention; think Eric Morecambe.

The following is a robust and ribald defense of Doggerel!

DOGGEREL

Ello !

Order Order!

God ordered Do-gooder

'Do Good Deed!

Do Glee!

Do Old Gold!

Do Droll…

Or Do Doggerel.'

Lo! Doggerel!

Doggerel 'Go Go Go!…'

Doggerel led,

Doggerel ogled, leered, rodgered Ego.

Doggerel Lorded,

Gored old Ego.

Doddle!

Good God!

Olé Doggerel

Olé Olé Olé!

George Gleddle

And on the subject of comedians, Bob Monkhouse once said, "People used to laugh at me when I said I wanted to be a Comedian. Well, they're not laughing anymore!"

Which is a good enough reason to take an interest in his career. Thus, I would like you to imagine, if you will, a young Bob, back in the 1950s, back in his small bedsit in Beckingham, Kent. He is pacing the floor, cravat slightly askew, in need of a shave, clad in cardigan and slacks, the de riguer of the times, dementedly puffing on his pipe, surrounded by rejected scripts, when, with a gleam in his eye, he suddenly stops to stare at himself in the mirror.

As he does so, he asks his reflection why it is, that despite all his efforts to be a comedian, he has never had that break he so desperately needs. He glares back at himself with an empty bottle of milk in his hand and then a slow smile appears on his face. The smile gets bigger until he smirks. Young Bob has just had an idea.

Bob has been part of the theatre crowd for some time and he has heard many of his thespian and writer friends wax lyrical about the Muse; that mythical and ethereal being who is said to come to aid the creative flow of those who request assistance in their creative endeavors. Young Bob thinks to himself that if it works for actors and writers, then it can also work for comedians.

Thus, Young Bob Monkhouse decides to contact his own Muse. The following is a word for word transcript of their communication. Although Bob became best known for his loquacity, the following verse reveals that Bob could also be Mr Brevity. Ergo, he communicated with his Muse using only the eight letters that appear in the word 'Comedian'. And the rest, as they say, 'is history'.

COMEDIAN

An Ode.

Young Bob:

O Iconic One.

I need Aid.

I'm doomed. I'm dammed.

I'm dim. I'm an Ommadon.

I'm an endemic enema encoded.

I concede I am a maniac

and a Demonic madman.

I need a Mind amended.

Muse:

O Comic One;

Mimic Mice and Men!

Young Bob:

O Come on Iconic One

Mimic Mice and Men?

No Man No!

I'm an MC.

I'm on a Mic

I need an M.O.

I need an Omen

I need Media

O Mend me, O Iconic One.

O, and can I add, I need an income.

Can I add, I demand...

I Command an income.

Muse:

O Come come, Comic One

I Mean 'Come On'.

I am a Meme

An Idiom.

I am a Dance; Dance in me,

Dance a Cancan!

Young Bob:

O Come on Iconic One

I can.

I mean I did.

I did dance a Cancan!

Muse:

O Come Come, Comic One

I am candid.

I am an idea.

I am Manna.

I Dance in Eden.

I Dance in Amen

In I 'n' I, I Dance.

I am a Named One

I am Om

I am in O C*OM*ic One.

I am O C*OMic* One.

Young Bob:

O

Mmmmmm

Ommmmmm

Om

O iconic one. I am Om.

I am a Comic One,

Moi!

"Thanks for that little history lesson Bri, The things you don't know until you know eh! And what about your own relationship with the Muse?", I almost hear you ask. "Is there anything you would like to share with us dear readers about this?"

Well, I do as it happens and so, as a wee respite from the One word Verse, here is an account of my personal first connection with the legendary Muse which suddenly came to me while bimbling past the Ledbury Mews.

THE MUSE

I assume a Muse is in me.

I assume I am in the Muse.

I assume a Muse amuses me

And I amuse the Muse.

"Amuse me, Muse", I say...

"I say I say I say" says the Muse,

"What's the News?"

And I say "It's new".

And the Muse says She Loves me

And I say

"I Love you too Muse".

And the Muse and me; we both Love the News.

"Thanks for sharing that snippet of information with us, Bri, into how your mind works at times. It was really informative. As I am sure you are aware, the burning question on all us dear readers' lips is,

'Just how long does it take you to dream up all these words of wit, wonder and wisdom and to then put pen to paper with such remarkable results?'

I am glad you asked me that question, but alas a lack of an answer precludes me from replying honestly. I can only say that it varies greatly but that the following verse is the one that took me the longest to create, for which the credit must go to the Muse.

PROCRASTINATION

A Pro Procrastination Oration.

To start,

Procrastination is not a sin

Nor is it Satanic.

So,

Procrastination is not a.s.a.p.

Nor is it Pronto.

It's not instant.

It's not " I can't"

Or an anti-start.

It is a start.

It's Procrastination!

It's not 'On 'n' on 'n' on'.

It's not static or still.

It's not a cast iron constant or a sprint into.

It's Procrastination!

So,

Is it an Inspiration?

It is 'n' it isn't!

Is it an Aspiration?

It is 'n' it isn't!

So, I Posit;

Procrastination is a trait,

It's an art.

It's a proposition to start;

at no cost to action.

It is Procrastination!

It's not in opposition to.

Procrastination is a Position.

It's Apt.

As a Notion, it coasts.

It's tops!

It's Procrastination!

So, start an Incantation

“Procrastination

Procrastination

Procrastination"

Start a Procrastination Nation.

Start it in Costa's.

Start it in Aston or in Costa Rica.

Start it anon.

Not too soon;

Cos it is

Procrast...

Innit!

" F-rippity f-rippity f-rip!" I almost hear you say. "This Muse seems a real Dude. She really does help writers! It all sounds really great, but we dear readers can't help but wonder if there are times when she doesn't like writers or how they write and so makes Herself scarce."

Hmm! A very good point and although I can't prove it, I suspect She has some reservations about page twenty-nine of the current Housing Benefit Form which states:

'Plain English Campaign's Crystal Mark does not cover this page'.

I am quietly confident that you will all recognise that this information has led me to ponder over the nature of Plain English and thus, you won't be in the least bit surprised, or put out, to discover that I have some thoughts on the matter which I am more than happy to share with you all.

PLAIN ENGLISH

Plain English is a pain.
Plain English is appalling.

Spanglish ees espgial
Shangaian Spiel is appealing
Alpen is legal Gashpalpen
Ships slang is a splish splash.
Plain English is appalling!

In Nepalese Pali
“Shegpan gilesh nigini paps
apsa pai pai pai”
is "As eggs is eggs is eggs
Plain English is an appalling lapse;
Alas, is poo poo anal."

Singhalese is all a singing.
Ghanaian is engaging.

Ipialanhi is a gaga gala
Lappish is a happening.
Shenanigan is a Gallig gig.
Plain English is appalling

Legensees glean in Asia.
Senegalese senses Sensei.
Shnaps slaps shlapen.
Ingalians ingale in silliness.
Plain English is appalling!

All in all,
A plea!
Plain English; Please gain in elan.
Ppp-please spell English
" SShhhhh! I E-n-g-l-i-s-e!"
As Plain English is appalling.

PS
“Ish”

"Crikey! What a dude this Muse is. Have you got any more One Word Verse words of wit wonder and wisdom?" I almost hear you say!

As it happens dearest readers, I do! Lots and lots but I can't possibly squeeze them all into this little book. There will be other books of course or you could always pop into the Spoken Word I host every week at the Abbey Road Coffee! But for now, here's one dedicated to Tom who owns and runs the ARC. Tom is also a top dude and a Beatles head to boot.

THE BEATLES

Stale?

Hate blah blah blah?

Hate labels?

Blast these blasted hassles!

Beat the blase!

Beat the beatless bleats!

Beat all the balls!

Beat the bells the bells the bells!

Hells Bells!

Tell a tale.
Tell a tall tale.
Beat the bells the bells the bells!

A la
Be a tease.
Eat the hat.
Eat the tea.
Eat the table's best assets.
Taste the last that the Beatles ate.
Eat the Beatles.
Tease the Bells the Bells the Bells!

Test the Bells.
Settle.
See the Bells heal.
See as all Bells heal.
As that'll be the Beatles.

See the Beatles as a table.

See a table as the Beatles.

See it all as a tete a tete.

As a tete a tete 'll

beat the Bells the Bells the Bells!

As all's a tete a tete;

Let all Bless all.

Let all sate all.

Let All et al be the Beatles.

La la la la la

Ah Bless!

Tee hee hee!

In anybody's language, that was pretty funky, wouldn't you agree, Lovelies? And such a bold flourishing of the much-maligned apostrophe too.

"Flourishing of the much-maligned Apostrophe, Bri?"

Oh well, you can't please everybody. Mustn't grumble though, coz here's one you'll definitely like. Remember Michaela? Yep, that's the one! Well, I was in Worsaucester a while back and I found myself in Cafe Bliss for the first time. I was writing a letter to her and can vividly remember jotting down something along the lines of;

'If I was ever asked to design a cafe, I would design it exactly like the one I have just wandered into.'

Which might not be the most imaginative of thought processes but it did elicit a response from the pen and paper I had with me at the time. And if memory serves me right, this is what it was.

CAFE BLISS

A Fable;

Alas, I ail.

Life baffles.

I flail.

As all else fails, I call a cab.

"Cafe Bliss" I blab.

I access Cafe Bliss.

I assess, feel Cafe Bliss.

I face Life's fallacies.

I face life's fibs, life's faeces.

I feel ease.

I feel able.

Affable, I abseil life.

I sail life's seas.

Celebs, Fellas, Lasses, Babes, Libbies, all.

All Liaise.

All Bless Cafe Bliss.

All Bless Ace, Fab ,Bella Bella Cafe Bliss.

All be Cafe Bliss.

All Be All.

Yep, I thought you'd like that one. It's always cool 'n groovy to spread your wings a little and make the delightful journey from Really Great Malvern station into Worsaucester and then raise thine eyes unto the hills on the return journey, but let's get back to Abbey Road Coffee shall we?

'Yes, but could we have another bit of a respite from the One Word Verse please Bri. We don't mean to be rude nor nufffing but…'

Fair enough my Lovelies! (There was a fairy. Her name was Nuff; Fairynuff) because here's a great little story about the Abbey Road Coffee that isn't One Word Verse.

Josh, another Barista Beau and lead singer with the White Feather Collective, was clearing up after a Spoken Word evening and was still wearing the wristband he'd got from the Glastonbury Festival two weeks previously. The two of us got talking about how we can, somehow, capture the essence of a place sometimes, and, seemingly, be able to hold on to that energy. We talked of Josh's feelings about Glastonbury and how I feel about the Abbey Road Coffee and the Spoken Word evenings. This, not unnaturally, got me to pondering about lingering, with the result that I read out the following verse the next week. And so, I dedicate this verse to Josh Lambe or…

All shall Heal

Jobbble Jobble Boom

Jah Jah Jah!

LINGERING

Not loitering, not lurking.

Glastonbury and ARC, Lingering.

Lingering;

on my clothes, my hair my face.

This lingering feeling reigning supreme.

Lingering.

Something lingering stays with me.

Don't wanna change my clothes, my hair, my face.

Glastonbury, ARC, capturing that feeling;

That Ingredient x,

That Lingering.

We're all the way we are because of our pasts.

Can't argue with that.

The ARC, Glastonbury, Lingering.

We sowed the seeds for our Lingering

When we were Lingering.

Lingering with Kindred Spirit,

There's no longing,

There's only now,

Only Lingering.

A smile in my heart as I am Lingering.

Happy to leave now and Linger elsewhere

Knowing I know who I am

Because of this heart that is Lingering.

And then the next week I read out the following verse because, such is the nature of our mind, that these feelings are impermanent.

Lingering Love.

Lingering doubts.

Lingering dust.

Lingering lust.

Lingering melancholics.

O Bollix!

Which, in its own inimitable style, is one way of explaining why I live at the Buddhist Temple in Really Great Malvern, strive to be a Buddhist and seek to understand more fully the nature of Impermanence. And such is the synchronicity and serendipity of life, that here is some One Word Verse that has just presented itself to me which reflects the nature of this search.

UNDERSTAND

Dear Dude;

A tete a tete.

Need a test?

Arsed?

Dare attend a date

and trade dread and drear.

Enter as a seed rare;

Start as an antenna.

Taste and test.

Saunter.

Strut a tad!

Started?

Add assets.

See stars and suns set.

See Auras.

Trust an Attendant as true;

as utter trust.

Attune!

Dread and drear are asunder; are dead.

Surrender!

Attest.

Stunned?

Sure?

Rest assured. Rest sated.

E'er assured; E'er sated.

Eer sussed; E'er treated.

Understand?

To understand is certainly a biiiiiiigy, but maybe by undoing all our conditioning, and with a helping hand from a Higher Source, it is possible. And if it is possible for one person, why not everybody? And so this next verse is dedicated to re-educating or re-minding ourselves.

EDUCATION

Attention Dude!

I indicate an odd Idea.

I announce an odd Intention.

I cue a notion.

I can undo it.

I can untie Education.

I can undo it and

Entice an Induction.

I conduct an Incantation.

A nod.

No contention.

I and Education attend a nuanced initiation and enact in inundated

Intention Intention Intention.

At once, an Attendant attended

And anointed it

And connected I and Education

on and on and on

in an intact connection.

Indeed in an on and on and on.....

Intended, innate, connected,

contented Education.

Done it Dude!

Done it.

Ace Innit!

Adieu Dude!

Anon.

As you may have gathered, the Abbey Road Coffee is staffed by lots of Lovelies, quite a few of whom have also lived at the Temple, which says a lot about both places. 0ne Temple Dweller and Abbey Road Coffee frequenter, as both Spoken Word Orator and daytime sipper of even more healthy drinks than the Cappuccino is Ana Maria; a young Lovely who arrived in Really Great Malvern on a One-way ticket from her homeland, Romania. Ana Maria catapulted herself into the Spiritual Path in Really Great Malvern before leaving on a One Way ticket for

Luxemburg. She is one of the most extraordinary people I have ever met and the following verse, 'Romania', is dedicated to her.

ROMANIA

Ami,

I am Ana Maria.

I am in Romania.

I am a Roma.

I Roam.

No room in Romania.

No Rain. No Moon.

"No room. No room in Romania," I roar.

O, I roar!

In Romania, I ran.

I ran in Romania.

In mania, I, Ana Maria, ran.

In a mirror, I ran.

I am in a mirror.

No! No! No!

I am a Mirror!

I am Ana Maria.

I am an Aria.

I am Manna.

I am Ana Maria.

I am Amora.

Mama Mia!

I am a Mirror.

I am Ana Maria.

I am Amora.

Namo* Amora.

Om Mani* Ana Maria

Ram Ram Rama Ram*

*Namo- I surrender my Love- Sanskrit

*Om mani –(Sanskrit) Often the first 2 words in Buddhist mantras which relate to the move from impurity to purity. The translation largely depends, however, on who you ask and when you ask them.

Ram ram rama ram. - God- Repeating the name of God (A Hindu mantra- Sanskrit).

Which, in anybody's language, my Lovelies, is a hard act to follow. Mustn't grumble though, because the next verse is right up there alongside it. It is dedicated to Maria Chippendale, another Spoken Word Orator, daytime sipper of the pot of tea and such like at the ARC and also the hostess of 'Sharing the Love', a gathering of souls for discussion of all things existential.

SHARE THE LOVE

There are those Orators, who, over the eras, relate tales. These Orators are Healers that resolve to share tales so that the heart heals; so that the heart oversees.

These Healers aver that these tales reverse hate;

that the tales verses are a theatre to alert, to treat the heart, so that the heart resolves to share.

The Healers share these tales to hearts

that travel here,

that travel there,

that rove,

that hover.

Healers share these tales so that the heart evolves.

The Orators stress that these tales

revere the heart

so that later, over eras,

the heart reveals a trove;

a trove rare, a trove overt.

There are those too, that stress that these tales trace a tear to the heart so that the heart

eases tears,

releases tears,

severs the tears,

so that the heart reveals Love.

So,

A toast to the tears.

A toast to those that revere these velvet tears.

A toast to the Healers that serve the heart.

So,

The heart stores Love.

So, restore Love.

Retreat to the heart to hear these tales.

Relate to these tales so that

the heart alters,

so that the heart shatters,

So that that the tales are the Hearts' altar.

Relate to the tales so Love

Ever salves

Ever lasts,

Ever sates,

Ever saves.

So...Start here, start here, start here.

Tell a tale.

Share the Love.

" F-rippity f-rippity f-rippity f-rip Bri!"

F-rippity f-rip Indeedy My Lovelies. It's all about timing and so it's about time that this first volume of One Word Verse gently closes its doors in order to allow other doors to open. And talking of which, it would be very rude of me not to mention the door of Aspects, the publisher of this wee tome.

I had been threatening to put together some of the verses for many a time when I happened upon Aspects which is located, believe it or not, right here in Really Great Malvern. This is the notice I read on the front door of the building and the rest, as they say, is staring you in the face.

ASPECTS

This is a Printing Office,

crossroads of civilisation,

refuge of all the Arts against the ravages of time.

From this place, words must fly abroad;

not to perish as walls of sound, but fixed in time,

not corrupted by the hurrying hand,

but verified in proof.

Friend, you are on safe ground.

You are in a printing office.

Beatrice Ward

'Irresistible' my Lovelies; 'Irresistible! ' And so it was that I went in and , not so very long after, Aspects published these words of wit, wonder and wisdom. And so it is too, my Lovelies, that I was inspired to ponder over the inherent meaning of this word 'Aspects' and wonder, in my own little way, if seeds of overcoming fear have been planted and left to scatter to the winds.

ASPECTS

At sea?

A tete a tete appt!

See a seascape.

Peep, access.

Assess Aspects.

See Aspects as a test.

Taste,

Step apace a.s.a.p.

Escape.

See as Aspects sees.

See Aspects as a state.

See Aspects as Peace.

See Aspects as Ease;

As Ace.

Attest as Aspects acts.

State;

" Aspects Sates"

Check this one out though before I go, my Lovelies. This was written by Maria. Yep, that's the one. She wrote a poem about my poems and every single word in it starts with one of the 10 different letters that appears in the poem 'Brian's Poems'.

"Eh?"

Check it out My Lovelies! Check it out!

BRIAN'S POEMS

Brian's poems are an Inspiration;
Enigmatic encounters of creation.
Perfecting prolific ponderings,
emanating soft,
musing on a Muse, sighing.
Brian's Poems, reminiscent of singing
melt moments.
Emotions streaming, seeming shy,
softly saunter,
Orating assurances of Omnipresence.

Brian's Poems, spoken in measured mazes,
mesmerise.
Slowly, reality moves.
Streams of silent particles murmur.

A Star, shining bright, sublime, escapes reality,
Pressing, Pulsating, Pausing...

Brian's Poems see people, places,

prophetically pondering on mysterious notions

not spoken.

Reality pauses plump at Beauty's Bounty

And by and by

All are inspired

Awe inspired

By Brian's poems.

I do have to go now and I am aware that it is pretty darned difficult to follow that, but here's a couple of naughty shorties that might just hit the spot.

MUSICIAN

Music is in us 'n' I am in music.

TOBY WREN (RGM Musician)

To Be or not to Be

or,

Not to worry!

And so, my Lovelies, a special thank you to all at Abbey Road Coffee, Aquarius, the Malvern Bookshop and Hunky Dorey, the four shops along the passage going from the steps and leading down to the Priory.

And a special heartfelt thanks to everybody who has come to the Spoken Word evenings, orators and listeners alike. The sense of warmth and welcome here has created a space where people have been able to feel safe and to express themselves; sometimes for the first time in their lives. They, as we all are, are on the path of overcoming fears and it is because of places such as the ARC where kindred spirits gather and healing happens, in which ever form this manifests, that our world becomes a slightly better place.

And a final special thanks to Annie from Hunky Dorey for the gift of the beautiful warm cardigan that will keep an elderly gentleman snug throughout wintry times while he sips on his cappuccino outside the ARC and embraces.

Namo Amida Bu my Lovelies.

I dedicate all virtues to Great Enlightenment.

Brian Graham

ABOUT THE AUTHOR

At present, Brian Graham is a Temple dweller at the Amida Mandala Buddhist Temple in Really Great Malvern and he frequents Abbey Road Coffee most days for a Cappuccino or two.

Afterward

" Thanks Bri. That was a such a Lovely book. Anyway, we all feel a bit more inspired than before we read it and so we thought we would join in the spirit of things. And so it is that it is that all of us Lovelies have got together and created a dedication to 'Spoken Word'. Any chance of printing it in your next volume of words of wit, wonder and wisdom Bri. Oh, go on Bri! Pleeeease! Goooooo on!"

'Let'see!' as a wise person once said. No, Only joking. I can't think of a good enough reason not to squeeze it in here right at the end. Let's see it then!'

SPOKEN WORD

Now Now!

Order Order!

S.O.S.

Sod rows.
Sod sorrows.
Depend on words.

Depend on prose.
on odes,
on words new,
on words reknown or worser.
Swoon on words,
so words prosper
Proper proper prosper.

Open doors.
Open words.
Poke words.
Re- order words.
Know words.
Pose.

Pen words
Own words
Own own words

Swoon on words
so words prosper, proper proper prosper.
Swoon on words
so words woo Eden,
So soon, words 'n' Eden powwow,
So, soon, Eden 'n' words wed.
So soon, Eden 'n' words send Word;
Send Word ‘Wow’.
So now, Eden owns words.
Words own Eden, own Now.
So now, Now owns Now;
Now's won.
So now, Now's won,
words prosper,
Proper proper poo.’
Poo?????

Er, Ooops! Sos!

So now, words proper proper prosper!

So now, spoken word proper proper prospers....

.....'n' so on....

O.K?

Spoken Word!!!

Oh thank you so much My Lovelies. Your words of wit, wonder and wisdom have made an elderly gentleman so very very happy!